Endorsements for *Lasting Words: A Guide to Finding Meaning Toward the Close of Life*

Claire Willis has written a psychologically wise and spiritually evocative guide for patients coming to the end of their lives. Through a combination of astute psychological advice, guided reflection and meditation, poetry, and prose, she lays out a path for people to find peace, connection, and meaning in this difficult period of life.

—SUSAN BLOCK, M.D., Chair, Department of Psychosocial Oncology and Palliative Care, Dana Farber Cancer Institute; Professor of Psychiatry and Medicine, Harvard Medical School and Co-Director of the Harvard Medical School Center for Palliative Care

Lasting Words offers us a delicately crafted guide, providing strong, secure scaffolding for the journey of living while dying, dying while living.

—REVEREND JULIA DUNBAR, M.DIV, Director of Pastoral Care and Education, Beth Israel Deaconess Medical Center, Boston, MA

What a treasure this simple and profound book is to those nearing the end of their life as well as to pastors, rabbis, chaplains and others who accompany them in the process!

—BRITA GIL AUSTERN, Philip Guiles Professor of Psychology and Pastoral Theology, Andover Newton Theological School, Newton, MA

Lasting Words is a gift to all people facing the end of life, their loved ones and those that care for them. Whether dying, or accompanying those who are dying, this book is a simple, practical guide to a very profound journey. I strongly recommend this for patients, families, and professional caregivers.

—CHRISTINA PUCHALSKI, M.D. M.S., Director and professor, George Washington Institute for Spirituality and Health; Professor of Medicine and Health Sciences at George Washington University; Author of *Time for Listening and Caring and Making Healthcare Whole;* Co-editor of *Oxford Textbook of Spirituality in Healthcare*

Lasting Words is both compassionate and wise. Claire has created a guide that will ease every reader's final journey. The reflections, examples, and quotations are as elegant and moving as her writing.

> —RACHAEL FREED, Author of *Your Legacy Matters,* and *Women's Lives, Women's Legacies: Creating Your Ethical Will*

Lasting Words is a gift that many of our patients and families are waiting for, providing a path through life's most difficult time as well as providing a source of comfort. Through meditations and writing exercises, we journey to what is most healing for ourselves. We are grateful for this new vital resource that will serve so many.

> —KOSHIN PALEY ELLISON & ROBERT CHODO CAMPBELL, Co-Founders of the New York Zen Center for Contemplative Care for the Dying

This is a thoughtful, gentle, and very helpful guide to a difficult time of life. Contemplating and writing about one's life may help shape the last days in a profound way that will soothe the writer and comfort the survivors.

> —HESTER HILL SCHNIPPER, LICSW, BCD and OSW-C, Chief of Oncology Social Work at Beth Israel Deaconess Medical Center, Boston, MA; Author of *After Breast Cancer: A Commonsense Guide to Life after Treatment* and *Woman to Woman: A Handbook for Women Newly Diagnosed with Breast Cancer*

Claire Willis has written a book of exquisite sensitivity, compassion and respect for the end of life journey. *Lasting Words* is a wise companion for those writing the last chapter in the book of their lives.

> —KATHLEEN ADAMS, LPC, Director, Center for Journal Therapy, Author, *Journal to the Self,* and others

Lasting Words is a "must" for end-of-life practitioners as well as those on their own healing journeys through illness.

> —NANCY BARCELOU, Director of Volunteers, VNA Hospice of Eastern Massachusetts

LASTING WORDS

A Guide to Finding Meaning
Toward the Close of Life

LASTING WORDS

A Guide to Finding Meaning Toward the Close of Life

CLAIRE B. WILLIS, LICSW

foreword by
JOAN HALIFAX

photographs by
MARNIE CRAWFORD SAMUELSON

Printed in the United States.

10 9 8 7 6 5 4 3 2 1

Green Writers Press is a Vermont-based publisher whose mission is to spread a message of hope and renewal through the words and images we publish. Throughout we will adhere to our commitment to preserving and protecting the natural resources of the earth. To that end, a percentage of our proceeds will be donated to the environmental activist group, 350.org. We will also give a percentage of our profits from this project directly to Vermont-based environmental organizations. Green Writers Press gratefully acknowledges support from individual donors, friends, and readers to help support the environment and our publishing initiative.

Giving Voice to Writers Who Will Make the World a Better Place
Green Writers Press | Brattleboro, Vermont
www.greenwriterspress.com

Library of Congress Cataloging-in-Publication Data is available upon request.

ISBN: 978-0-9899838-0-8

COVER & BOOK DESIGN BY CAROLYN KASPER
PHOTOS © 2013 MARNIE CRAWFORD SAMUELSON www.bostonpicturegroup.com
FRONT COVER PHOTO © ALISON SHAW www.alisonshaw.com

Permissions to use the poems reprinted in this book appear on page 125.

PRINTED WITH SOY-BASED INKS ON PAPER MADE FROM PULP THAT COMES
FROM POST-CONSUMER WASTE PAPER IN A FAMILY-OWNED, FSC®-CERTIFIED
PRINTER, LOCATED IN VERMONT UTLIZING RESPONSIBLE ENVIRONMENTAL,
SOCIAL, AND ECONOMIC PRACTICES. MADE WITH A CHLORINE-FREE
APROCESS (ECF: ELEMENTAL CHLORINE FREE).

For Alex and Margaret,
whose words are lasting

CONTENTS

PREFACE

T HE INTRODUCTION of this powerful book is "Your Words Matter." And so this guide unfolds a path for bringing narrative, language and words to a world that is often met by muteness or distraction.

In this carefully and beautifully crafted text, you will find a treasure house of word-based guidance through the journey of illness. It is almost always true that sickness surfaces the deep need for meaning in our lives. Our priorities shift as we see the horizon of life that is the threshold of death. The practice of expressing gratitude, love, forgiveness, of the discovery of long held but rarely expressed values, the hidden stories that percolate in the final months of life, and the chance to share all this with wise and compassionate others changes the landscape of dying and opens the door to living more fully, honestly, bravely, and richly.

Writing is a practice and path, and this guide gives us a tool to bring forth the treasures in the mind and in the heart that have long remained out of sight. Meditation, relaxation, writing practice, working with gratitude, hope, forgiveness, wisdom and endings can be the way signs on the journey that bring us to the close of life.

Having such a guide as this is immensely valuable to all of us. Whether we use it for ourselves or share it with another, it is a path to a richer life that gives meaning to us and to those around us as our journey takes us to the unknown.

—JOAN HALIFAX,
author of *Being With Dying*

Author's Note

For the last 20 years, I have had the privilege of leading writing groups for people living with cancer and their loved ones. I could not have imagined or anticipated the healing impact that writing could have, both for the writers and for those receiving and reading their words. People living with a life threatening disease often share common questions and concerns: How will I be remembered? What difference has my life made and what difference is it making right now? How do I pass on my values and life lessons to my family and loved ones? How do I share some of the lessons I learned to help reduce the suffering of others? What legacy will survive me? Writing about these intimate concerns offers an opportunity for solace, healing and closure.

Lasting Words is a collection of reflections, meditations, poetry, quotations and writing exercises that I have used in my group work over the past years. The work of the writing group members at both The Wellness Community and Facing Cancer Together in Newton, Massachusetts is featured throughout the book. I am eternally grateful to those who entrusted me with their presence and who shared their writing with the group. I have included work by group members throughout the book. In some instances, I have excerpted their pieces. At other times, the writing appears in its original form. I have changed writers' names to respect their privacy.

This book started out as a graduate program thesis requirement. Roshi Joan Halifax, one of the first readers and one of my teachers, immediately envisioned my thesis as a book, and encouraged me to publish it. I am grateful for her vision. In the initial stages, Marnie Crawford Samuelson, my good friend and photographer, along with Dan Wallace, reviewed every word I wrote with much care and discerning eyes. My friends—Abe Feingold, Lisa McDonnell, Rachael Freed, Julia Dunbar, Margaret Metzger, Marilyn and Bob Kriegel—and both my daughters, Carlin and Emily Greenstein, collectively spent hours reading and commenting on the first few drafts of the manuscript, helping to bring it into readable shape! Mia Jacobson-Miller toiled for hours with the poetry permissions. I couldn't have chosen a better colleague. Alison Shaw generously allowed us to use her photograph on the front cover of *Lasting Words*.

The designer, Carolyn Kasper, grasped and believed in the spirit of this book from the beginning. I am thankful for her vision, patience and guidance. She has created a book that is not only beautiful, but a gentle and open-hearted invitation to the reader. I am delighted to be working with Dede Cummings, the founder of Green Writers Press. I respect the bold mission of her press and so appreciate her enthusiastic embrace of this book. And finally, a very special thanks to my editor Susan Suffes who really knew how to make lemonade from lemons and believed in the book from the start. She offered a steady hand at every turn.

LASTING
WORDS

A Guide to Finding Meaning
Toward the Close of Life

INTRODUCTION

YOUR WORDS MATTER

PERHAPS WORDS never matter more than they do at the end of life. For the past 20 years, I have led writing groups for people with life-threatening diseases. I have seen up close the healing power of words, both for the writer and for those receiving their words. People with only days or months to live want to explore spiritual issues and engage in a search for the deeper meaning of their lives. Using writing for that exploration offered them a particular kind of solitude to sort through their most personal thoughts and feelings.

The search for meaning and purpose at the end of life is universal. We all seek comfort and strength as we close our lives. When we become sick, we begin to let go of roles that previously offered significance, status and definition. These include our job titles, our position and responsibilities in the family, other offices and affiliations. As we lose these ways of thinking about ourselves, we seek new meaning—a larger worth—informed by internal rather than external concerns. How we work with these losses and still find meaning will shape and inform how we close our lives.

The last year of life provides unexpected opportunities for growth and healing. People often say to me, "While I would not wish to have cancer, I am grateful for the gifts that it has brought me." I have seen many people open to wisdom they always possessed but couldn't see until they became ill. Perhaps you are now aware of a need to feel that you belonged or that you wanted to be known more than you feel you are right now. Maybe there is a yearning to want the people you know and love to remember you and to feel that your time on earth actually made a difference to them. These are common and universal feelings and needs that individuals often begin to experience as they age and approach the end of their lives.

I wrote this guide to help people find meaning, to provide comfort and to offer strength. When people are at or near the end of life, they may turn to writing as a way of speaking to loved ones to address unresolved questions and as a means of offering a gift or legacy to those they are leaving behind. The words from these days may be the most valuable gift that can be given by individuals who are dying, a window into themselves that perhaps they were never able to share. You'll read about the lasting words of people with whom I worked throughout this book.

There are limitless ways to leave a part of who you are in written form. Maybe you want to tell loved ones about important moments or experiences from your life, about what matters and has mattered to you, about who you are. Maybe you want to write letters to your children, family members or friends about your memories and about how you wish to be remembered. Maybe there is a letter of forgiveness you might choose to write to a friend.

Our words are a gift to ourselves as well. They can provide comfort, a way of sorting out what we think and feel. Even if we don't finish, even if no one else reads them, they are an affirmation of our life.

Each chapter focuses on one of the spiritual issues of common concern: Our Journey, Gratitude, Hope, Forgiveness, Wisdom, Prayer, and Endings. Within the chapters are invitations to reflect on writing, relaxation exercises, poetry, quotations, refective questions and closing meditations. The selections of poetry and quotations are included to help stimulate your thinking, access a memory or take you to deeper feelings.

A PERSONAL JOURNAL

Sometimes you may want to keep your written reflections to yourself. At other times, you might want to use them to send or share with someone. Perhaps you will want to leave some writing as a legacy to your loved ones. That is up to you.

This book may have come to you through a chaplain, or maybe a friend handed it to you and suggested that you try the exercises in it. Perhaps you just discovered it in the facility where you receive medical care. No matter how it came to you, it took courage for you to pick it up. It took strength, a willingness, curiosity, and courage to consider finding the words to write about who you are along with some of your deepest concerns and truths.

Lasting Words can be used alone or with others. It is as comforting as a contemplative process as it is an interactive one. It is my deepest hope that it will serve as a healing tool in assisting you in reaching for the ultimate meaning in your life as you begin to say goodbye.

"May God keep you safe 'til the word of your life is fully spoken."

—Irish Blessing

PART ONE

FIRST STEPS

CHAPTER ONE

BEFORE YOU BEGIN

Writing can seem daunting, and one of the biggest challenges is figuring out how to begin. So let's start with the basics. Here are a few simple things that people have found to be useful:

Buy a journal and pen or pencil or ask someone to get them for you

- Take a moment to personalize your journaling experience. Decide whether you would like lined or plain paper, a pad or a spiral-bound book, large or small.
- What type of writing instrument do you prefer—roller ball, pencil or ballpoint? Some people choose to write on a computer. However, many people find that pressing keys on a keyboard is a different experience than keeping a journal with pen and paper.

If you are mobile, choose a quiet peaceful place to write

- If you are in bed, set the blinds the way you would like them to be and make sure the pillows around you are arranged in a comfortable way.

To the extent it is possible for you, set aside time on a daily basis that you dedicate to yourself so that you begin to strengthen the habit of reflecting and writing

- Try to block off about 20 minutes a day, preferably when you wake up or after a nap. If you can't manage 20 minutes, try setting aside a shorter time period, but have a goal.
- Maintain a daily practice, preferably at the same time each day, as this is a powerful way to strengthen your writing.
- As you make physical space in your life to write, you may well find that more and more memories come forth. When you make and keep appointments between your heart and your writing, something will emerge and begin to happen, often in surprising and unexpected ways.
- Keep your journal private. Put it in a secure place that no one else knows about. Unless you feel confident about the confidentiality of your journal, you may begin to censor and modify what you write, and this may cause your writing to be other than authentic and heartfelt.

Getting started is usually the most difficult part. Congratulations for getting this far. Remember that you picked up this book for a reason. Be patient and gentle with yourself.

CHAPTER TWO

RELAXATION
AND MEDITATION

STARTING OUT each chapter with a relaxation exercise will help you enter the process of reading and reflecting with more ease and openness. When stressed, it's hard to think clearly. By starting with the following exercise at the beginning of each chapter, you will be more responsive to the reflections, quotations and poetry that follow. By repeating the exercise throughout the book, you may find that you can remember it and use it in other potentially stressful situations. These might include such things as waiting to hear medical news or writing with pain and discomfort.

RELAXATION

Come into a comfortable seated position in a chair or in your bed, with your spine upright and as straight as you are able to make it. If you are seated in a chair, place your feet flat on the floor and allow your hands to rest gently in your lap, the palms gently touching your belly.

Allow your eyes to close, or look toward the floor. If there is no one else present to read these written instructions to you, read them to yourself.

As you draw your attention to the contact of the bottom of your feet with the floor, or your heels with the bed, your buttocks against your seat, and your spine against the cushions behind you, let your body relax into those points of support.

Gently press down into the sitting surface, feeling the spine lift slightly, broadening your collarbone and feeling the verticality of your spine. Say to yourself, "strong back." Feel the strength of your spine. This mental engagement deepens your capacity to relax.

If your condition does not allow you to feel a strong spine, just imagine it.

Allow your awareness to come to the front of your body and soften the muscles around your eyes, jaw and mouth. Allow your shoulders to drop down and shoulder blades to slide down your back. Relax the palms of your hands, letting go of any tension or tightness that might be there.

Bring your awareness to your belly and as you breathe in, see if you can allow the muscles of your belly to relax and open, to soften. You will notice as you do this that on the inhalation the belly seemingly fills and expands with air, and as you exhale the belly draws back toward the spine. On each in breath, say to yourself, "soft front" or "soft belly."

As you settle into feeling the movement of breath and its impact on the front of your body, say to yourself, "strong back, soft front." Link your mind to the movement of your body and breath, bringing your mind, body, and breath together. Observe the continuous flow of the breath for a few moments. When your mind wanders, gently bring it back to the united movement of body and breath, saying to yourself, "strong back, soft front (or soft belly)."

After a few moments, draw in a couple of long deep soft breaths and let your awareness return to the room, slowly opening your eyes. Now you are ready to begin the chapter.

MEDITATION

Just as you begin a chapter with a relaxation exercise to open to your thoughts and feelings, close it with a meditation to bring a sense of peace to whatever reflection or writing you have done. There are different meditations for each chapter. All should be done like this:

Sit quietly for a few moments.

Settle into noticing your breath and say to yourself, "strong back, soft front (or soft belly)." Link your mind to the movement of your body and breath. If your condition does not allow you to feel a strong spine, just imagine it.

Observe the continuous flow of breath.

Then, on each out breath, say one phrase of the meditation. For instance, for "Your Journey," the pattern would be:

(Out breath)   *May I be free of fear*
(Out breath)   *May my life be of service*
(Out breath)   *May I be remembered with love*
(Out breath)   *May I find inner peace*

Silently repeat the first phrase three times to yourself and then move on to the second phrase, again reciting that to yourself three times. When you have completed all four phrases and recited each of them three times, just pause for a moment.

As you close the meditation, slowly and gently let your attention return to the room.

CHAPTER THREE

GETTING STARTED

Choose a chapter

- Review the sequence of chapters and notice what you are drawn toward or what speaks to your concerns.
- While it isn't necessary to do the chapters in any particular order, many people have found that starting with the chapter "My Journey" generated ideas for the subsequent chapters.
- Begin each writing session with a relaxation exercise (see page 12).

Date each journal entry

- When you look back over what you have written, it's usually helpful to be able to place a piece of writing within the context of what may be going on in your life.

Begin to write and let the words come

- Write about your thoughts and feelings and the stories behind them.
- Allow yourself to relive emotional times and see if you can find the lesson in those difficulties.
- Give voice to different aspects of yourself—the child, the young adult, the sportsperson, the family member, the hobbyist, the dreamer—as well as the adult that you became.

Write truthfully

- Writing about what is true for you translates into an authentic voice and good writing.
- In the face of truth, pace yourself according to what you can tolerate and manage with ease, especially in the chapter on forgiveness.

Push through any hesitancy or reluctance you might feel

- You may feel you have nothing important to say or you don't know how to answer a question that is posed. That's normal, but try to keep going. Often people can get beyond these feelings when they keep writing.

- Jot down some notes or list whatever thoughts come to mind as you read each question. Writing might develop from the notes or list later on.

- You may find the number of questions in each chapter overwhelming, especially if you have limited energy. Simply choose one that seems to have meaning, work with it for a while, and then rest.

Try not to "should have" yourself

- It's natural to have expectations for yourself, but these expectations often lead to self-censorship and may cut off the flow of ideas. Just allow your thoughts to gather as they will and trust in yourself as you write.

- Don't worry about neatness, spelling or grammar; write what comes from your engaged mind and your open heart.

- Don't throw away anything that you write. You never know when, or if, you might want to re-read this material. There might be seeds of healing in it that you may wish to return to in the future.

- Read out loud to yourself what you write; you will hear the words differently. Sometimes what you intended to write actually never got on the page! You might also experience the delightful surprise of finding that you know something that you didn't think you knew.

Expect setbacks

- Fears are common and, I assure you, they are normal.
- Many people feel shy about their writing. Even seasoned writers admit to fear, especially in front of a blank sheet of paper. Maybe you were told (even as far back as elementary school) that you didn't know how to write. Maybe you thought you could write and then bumped up against some other obstacle and lost confidence. Maybe you never even tried to write. Whatever your history, right now you have an opportunity to express yourself. Use it.
- Be prepared to deal with a flood of discouraging thoughts. These might include:

  "I don't have time to write."

  "I don't have the energy to write."

  "I don't know what to write."

  "Who would ever want to read what I write anyway?"

  "And on top of all that, I am a terrible writer."
- Such thoughts arise naturally when you encounter new challenges and can stop the beginning of a project in its tracks. Try to stay focused on what is most important to you. Remember that periods of hesitancy or doubt are natural. We all experience them. Just try to keep on writing.

There are many writing suggestions offered in each chapter, more than anyone might want to take up. My hope is that by offering a wide variety of reflections, there will be a few that will touch you.

The most important thing to remember is to write from your experience and do so truthfully and from the heart.

"The bitterest tears shed over graves are for words left unsaid and deeds left undone."

—HARRIET BEECHER STOWE

PART TWO

⌒

SEVEN PATHS TO LASTING WORDS

CHAPTER FOUR

ON YOUR JOURNEY

"WHEN I heard that I should write about my journey, I thought, 'that's not me,'" Christina, a 45-year-old member of my writing group, told me. "I've never been anywhere exotic. Actually, that's an understatement. I've never been more than 20 miles from my hometown. It wasn't that I couldn't; I didn't want to. So, what could I tell about my journey? But when I started to write, I began to understand that it's not about the distance you go but rather about the experiences and perspectives you gain as you live your life. I saw that I could describe what I thought and felt that was both expected and unexpected. I could pass on what I learned about others and myself. In that way, I became a world traveler because I could tell about my world and my journey in it."

REFLECTIONS ABOUT YOUR JOURNEY

"Everyone must leave something behind when he dies," my grandfather said. "A child or a book or a painting or a house or a wall built or a pair of shoes made. Or a garden planted. Something your hand touched some way so your soul has somewhere to go when you die, and when people look at that tree or that flower you planted, you're there."

—RAY BRADBURY

Writing a story of your life is a wonderful way to create a legacy of who you have been in this lifetime. Through your life story, you make yourself known beyond whatever roles you played, whether it was as a parent, relative, teacher, doctor, nurse, janitor, clerk, manager, soldier or social worker—the list goes on.

Author Rachael Freed describes all the ways that writing a memoir or legacy helps us fulfill basic human needs. They include the wish to belong, to be known, to be remembered, to believe our life has made a difference, to bless and be blessed and to celebrate life.[1]

In writing your legacy, you define yourself through language and story. You can re-create yourself, reflecting back with a wisdom that was perhaps missing while you were living your day-to-day life. By creating and re-creating in your writing, you remind yourself that your life made a difference.

By reviewing your life in a focused way, you can recast the past and place it in the context of the present moment. Doing this on the threshold of losing your life, you may feel a deeper appreciation of what your life has been and you may want to celebrate it. You may realize how precipitously lives are shattered and how often the mundane details of life become sacred. The process of reflection provides new sources of meaning.

There are many ways to enter into a reflection of your life. One way is to reflect back on distinct periods like childhood, teenage years, or a specific time, say, between ages 30 and 40. What were the significant moments and events during that time? Who were the people who guided and influenced you? What did these experiences contribute to your life?

As you reflect, you may see patterns that were there all along but were invisible while you were busy living the moments that created them. Perhaps this writing process will help you find a new sense of gratitude for many of your experiences. If your life was difficult, perhaps you will appreciate the strengths you were forced to cultivate in order to survive.

Each person will enter into this creative process in ways that make sense to him or her. The questions below are simply guides for creating the story of your journey.

> *"We are lonesome animals. We spend all our life trying to be less lonesome. One of our ancient methods is to tell a story begging the listener to say—and to feel—'Yes, that's the way it is, or at least that's the way I feel it.' You're not as alone as you thought."*
>
> —JOHN STEINBECK

AN INVITATION TO REFLECT AND WRITE

*"The last great freedom of man is the freedom to choose
his attitude under any given set of circumstances."*
—VICTOR FRANKL

A gentle reminder: You don't have to answer all the questions or do all the exercises. Simply choose one or two that resonates with you, work with it for a while, and then rest.

Gathering memories and stories

- One approach is to think of your life in segments of seven years. Recalling memories in segments of time will often help you to remember more details. Recollect some of the significant personalities from each time period. Think about the people who were your guides or teachers, and how this phase of your life contributed to your life over all. Remember that even though you may not have known someone directly, the person may have affected your life deeply. Another approach is to brainstorm (list, without self-censorship, as many ideas as you can), sketch, doodle or scribble.

- There are many additional ways to stimulate the mind. Use family photos, drawings, literature, poetry, music or favorite books to jog your memory.

- As you recall various phases of your life, you might want to devote a page to each one. That way, it will be easy to add more reflections as you happen to think of them.

Sources of meaning

- What were the primary sources of meaning in your life? Consider work, love, creativity, service, humor, or nature. What, in these areas, gave your life meaning?

Turning points

Each of us faced times when we had to make important decisions including where to go to school, what work to do, where to live and whether to marry or have children.

- What were some of your critical choice points and what guided your decisions during those times?
- Reading Robert Frost's poem "The Road Not Taken" might be helpful in thinking about these changes.

The Road Not Taken

Two roads diverged in a yellow wood,
And sorry I could not travel both
And be one traveler, long I stood
And looked down one as far as I could
To where it bent in the undergrowth;

Then took the other, as just as fair,
And having perhaps the better claim,
Because it was grassy and wanted wear;
Though as for that the passing there
Had worn them really about the same,

And both that morning equally lay
In leaves no step had trodden black.
Oh, I kept the first for another day!
Yet knowing how way leads on to way,
I doubted if I should ever come back.

I shall be telling this with a sigh
Somewhere ages and ages hence:
Two roads diverged in a wood, and I—
I took the one less traveled by,
And that has made all the difference.

—ROBERT FROST

Values

A value is a belief, mission, or philosophy that means something to you. Sometimes we are very conscious of our values and at other times less so. Some values are basic, such as a belief in working hard, being on time, finishing what you set out to do or becoming as educated as you can. Others are more psychological, such as being self-reliant, attending to the needs of others and maintaining peace at any price.

• What values have been guideposts for you throughout your life? How were they evident and how did they shape important decisions and your daily life?

• What did you once consider important, but now view through a different lens?

Your name

All of us have been known by different names at times in our lives. We have names our family, our loved ones, or our enemies have called us. We have names a few select people know. We have names we call ourselves privately. We have names that relate to what we long for. Perhaps there is a name you yearned to call yourself, one that would offer a needed quality or strength in some trying circumstance.

• Make a list of all the names you remember being called. How did you come to acquire some of those names? Is there a story behind any of them that you might want to share with someone?

• Is there a name you need right now to accompany you on your journey, a name that might embody a quality for which you yearn?

Being remembered

- How do you hope to be remembered?
- What words would you hope that people might use to describe you?
- Try starting with this writing phrase: "I hope that people will say…"

Future generations

- Imagine a great-grandchild that you may never meet but who desires to know about you. What would you want him or her to know about you and about life in general?
- Are there specific stories or experiences that you want to share? What would you like to leave behind?

Lessons

- What three lessons have you learned in life, and what were the experiences that taught you those lessons?
- Are there lessons that you learned in a hard way that, by sharing your story and experiences, could spare others difficulty? (In the chapter on wisdom, there is an example of one way to do this exploration. See page 79.)
- Is there someone with whom you would like to share these stories right now?

Souvenirs

- A souvenir is an object of commemoration, a keepsake or a memento that reminds you of a time or an event. In the past, some of your souvenirs may have included ticket stubs, keys, a program from a concert or a love letter.
- What are the souvenirs of your life, the tokens by which you would want to be remembered, the things that represent your life?
- What might you want people to know about them and why you chose them?
- Are there specific mementos or keepsakes that you want to give particular people as a way to remember you?

You are more than memories—a caveat

Memories and the stories we tell each other give meaning to our lives and to the lives of others. But consider that memories are not everything. What you remember and what actually happened may be quite different. Memories are at best snapshots—a part of the truth, but incomplete.

> *"Inside of all of us there is the need and the desire to be heard, to have our innermost thoughts, feelings and desires expressed for others to hear, to see and to understand. We all want to matter to someone, to leave a mark. Writers just take those thoughts, feelings and desires and express them in such a way that the reader not only reads them but feels them as well."*
>
> —VICKTOR ALEXANDER

Wild Geese

You do not have to be good.
You do not have to walk on your knees
for a hundred miles through the desert, repenting.
You only have to let the soft animal of your body
     love what it loves.
Tell me about despair, yours, and I will tell you mine.
Meanwhile the world goes on.
Meanwhile the sun and the clear pebbles of the rain
are moving across the landscapes,
over the prairies and the deep trees,
the mountains and the rivers.
Meanwhile the wild geese, high in the clean blue air,
are heading home again.
Whoever you are, no matter how lonely,
the world offers itself to your imagination,
calls to you like the wild geese, harsh and exciting—
over and over announcing your place
in the family of things.

    —MARY OLIVER

The New Story of Your Life

Say you have finally invented a new story
of your life. It is not the story of your defeat
or of your impotence and powerlessness
before the large forces of wind and accident.
It is not the sad story of your mother's death
or of your abandoned childhood. It is not
even a story that will win you the deep
initial sympathies of the benevolent goddesses
or the care of the generous, but it is a story
that requires of you a large thrust
into the difficult life, a sense of plenitude
entirely your own. Whatever the story is,
it goes as it goes, and there are vicissitudes
in it, gardens that need to be planted,
skills sown, the long hard labors
of prose and enduring love. Deep down
in some long-encumbered self,
it is the story you have been writing
all of your life, where no Calypso holds you
against your own willfulness,
where there are no longer dark caves
for you to be imprisoned in,
where you can rise
from the bleak island of your old story
and tread your way home.

—MICHAEL BLUMENTHAL

"Our spiritual and religious lives depend on the stories we choose to tell and how we tell them."

—Sandy Eisenberg Sasso

CLOSING MEDITATION

May I be free of fear

May my life be of service

May I be remembered with love

May I find inner peace

CHAPTER FIVE

ON GRATITUDE

AFTER MY dear friend Alex was diagnosed with metastatic ovarian cancer, she told me that she was deeply grateful for her six grown children. Over the years she had kept all the letters her children had written her, from the times they were young, right through to adulthood. She made copies of all the letters, bound them, and gave the collection to each child. "My children are my legacy," she told me. "By sharing each one's thoughts with the others, I feel that I can step aside as head of the family. I want them to be able to connect with each other more deeply and what better way than to read what each sibling wrote to me? This way they all possess a written history of our life together. I'm so grateful that I can do this for them."

REFLECTIONS ABOUT GRATITUDE

"At times our own light goes out and is rekindled by a spark from another person. Each of us has cause to think with deep gratitude of those who have lighted the flame within us."

—ALBERT SCHWEITZER

We have all had moments of feeling grateful, blessed and fortunate. It's easy to conjure up these positive feelings when we are healthy, when it's a beautiful, warm, sunny day and when we are doing something we utterly love. It's especially easy to do when things are going our way.

But what about feeling truly thankful when things are not going the way we want them to or when we are in pain? What about when we feel hopeless and helpless, or when we have been sick for a long time?

Gratitude at those moments may seem impossible. The mere suggestion of it in the midst of some situations may feel irritating or infuriating. For someone to suggest that we could—or should—feel grateful in the face of our own adversity seems disrespectful.

When we are sick, our attention naturally goes toward what is difficult, painful or uncomfortable. Some of us default to old habits, like anger, depression, anxiety or withdrawal. Maybe these coping mechanisms served us well at some point in time. They may have even protected us but in the present, when we need strength and healing, they are no longer useful. What we may need now is calm and inner peace.

As we become conscious of our own mortality and of life's impermanence, we may try to find our way to feeling grateful—and appreciating *even* this time. Pema Chodron, a Buddhist teacher and author, reminds us to keep our heart and mind open and to welcome whatever comes into the circle of our life.[2] That kind of welcome includes all of our feelings whether they are happiness, sadness, anger, jealousy or whatever is present in us. It means deeply befriending our own self.

Consider the idea of "taking in the good," a phrase used by author Rick Hanson.[3] In the midst of pain and anguish, you can choose to turn your attention toward what is right, however small a gesture, detail, or fleeting moment that might be. By lingering for 10 to 30 seconds on whatever blessings are in your life, you can expand your capacity to handle difficulties and find inner peace. Perhaps a nurse or friend gently washed or massaged you, or someone brought flowers, or a meal was especially good, or the light came through the window at a lovely slant, illuminating the dust motes.

By remembering the good and holding it next to what is difficult, you can readily see how other people are responsible for the gifts of your life. When you feel entitled or take for granted whatever you have, it's not possible to see how other people enhance your life by their presence.

Consider for a moment where you are living, how you arrived there, who is taking care of you and what medications bring you comfort. Consider also smaller gifts like clean water that comes with the turn of a faucet, the light that goes on with the turn of a switch, or the comfort of clean sheets on your bed. These things exist because of the efforts of many people, like those who constructed the building, engineered efficient roads, researched medications, created water systems, wired your building for electricity and made your bed. What if you noticed the countless gestures and actions of people who make your days more graceful?

Taking in the good by allowing for moments of gratitude in the face of living with ongoing losses and impermanence helps us to build inner resilience in the face of our difficulties. Taking in the good and pausing to say "thank you" helps us remember those who have helped us in the past and those who continue to contribute toward making our lives easier in whatever conditions we find ourselves. The following exercises are intended to help you remember to take in the good and pause with it. Doing so will help balance your attention, holding the good alongside the losses.

> "Can you see the holiness in those things you take for granted—a paved road or a washing machine? If you concentrate on finding what is good in every situation, you will discover that your life will suddenly be filled with gratitude, a feeling that nurtures the soul."
>
> —HAROLD KUSHNER

AN INVITATION TO REFLECT AND WRITE

*"The miracle of gratitude is that it shifts your perception
to such an extent that it changes the world you see."*
—DR. ROBERT HOLDEN

A gentle reminder: You don't have to answer all the questions or do
all the exercises. Simply choose one or two that resonates with you,
work with it for a while, and then rest.

Gratitude journal

- Consider things in your life that make you feel happy (for example: talking with someone, seeing the sun through the clouds, enjoying people who visit, or feeling cared about).

- As you write about feeling grateful and appreciative, allow yourself to feel happiness in your body. Linger with the reflection as you write about it.

- At the end of a day, list five things that happened that day about which you feel grateful. It might be as simple as being greeted with a smile or receiving an unexpected visitor or phone call. Perhaps it was the sounds of birds outside the window or music on the radio.

- Use your senses to remember an unexpected sight, a sound, a pleasant scent, or a touch. It might even be the soothing sound of your own breath. Perhaps there was even a moment when you were able to do something you didn't think you could do.

- You might use these questions to help remember the day:

  What have I received today from _____?

  What have I given today to _____?

Morning prayers of gratitude

- As you wake up, visualize some positive events that might arise throughout the course of the day. Maybe it is a nap that will leave you rested or a sponge bath that will leave you feeling refreshed.

- Take two to three minutes to express gratitude—give thanks—for having a whole new day before you. If you wake up and do not feel grateful, remember Shakespeare's advice to "Assume a virtue if you have it not," often paraphrased as "Fake it until you make it." Research has shown that emotions often follow behavior. You cannot feign gratitude, but it's possible to behave "as if" you were grateful, thereby creating a space in which feelings of gratitude are more likely to emerge.

- Consider selecting a piece of writing that expresses gratitude and resonates with you and keeping it nearby. It might be a poem, a prayer, a reflection of your own or someone else's. Perhaps you can memorize something that has meaning for you. Look over the poems and quotations in this chapter to see whether any of them might help give language to a meaningful expression of gratitude for you.

Letters of appreciation and thank-you notes

- Realizing that you are living with a life-threatening situation, you may feel the desire to express appreciation to those people who helped you at various points in your life. Perhaps you met someone who changed your perspective at a critical time. Maybe someone offered some wisdom at a point where you were confused and overwhelmed. Or perhaps you experienced an intense encounter with someone, maybe a love affair, during a transitional period in your life that for some reason helped you over the threshold.

- Each of us knows people who, at one time or another, did an act of kindness or a favor or showed up at a critical moment when we needed help. Perhaps you were so fortunate to have someone as a steady presence in your life.

- Begin to think about these people. Remember when you were very young, maybe up to the age of 10. Then look at the next decade, your teenage years, and the decades after that. For each decade, write down the names of three people (or more if you choose) who you remember making a difference in your life and to whom you feel grateful and appreciative because their presence made a sustaining difference. The list might include a teacher, nurse, storekeeper, family member, friend, caretaker, sibling or other relative, doctor, coach or volunteer. Jot down some notes about what made them important, what they gave you and how their presence in your life made a difference. What did you appreciate about them?

- Choose one or more persons on that list, living or dead, about whom, or to whom, you might consider writing.

- One approach is to write about how these individuals were unique to you, what gifts they brought and how their presence affected you.

- Another approach would be to write directly to them. Perhaps you might want to express thanks for a gesture or an act. Hold nothing back and allow your heart to lead the way. This is a valuable opportunity to both strengthen the connections from your life and bring them to closure.

- You may choose to put these letters away when you complete them. Or you may decide to wait a while before you mail or send them to recipients. They can also be given to someone with instructions to be distributed at a later point in time. Its up to you.

Visual reminders

- Using visual reminders may be helpful in cultivating an attitude of gratitude. Try index cards attached to the wall in your room or in the kitchen, or a collage that you made, or gifts that someone gave you that instill a sense of gratitude.

- One commonly used saying is "Yesterday is history. Tomorrow is a mystery. Today is the present." Another is "Today is a gift."

Grateful intentions

- Create an intention to be grateful and reaffirm it each morning and throughout the day.

- Keep in mind when you are creating it that a supportive intention is short, simple and does not contain any negative words like "won't," "can't," "shouldn't," or "not." Realistic intentions and affirmations are easiest to work with. Feel the difference as you read these two intentions out loud:

  "I will not complain any more about everything that has gone poorly in my life."
  (This is too big an expectation, includes a negative word and is too long.)

  "For just this morning, I will focus on what is right."
  (This is short, simple and positive.)

Finding gold in the hard times

- Think back over your life and remember a difficult or challenging time. It might have been a friend's betrayal, a loss of a person or a pet, a divorce, or the unexpected loss of a job. Often these events, while initially devastating, bring unexpected lessons, insights, or gifts into our lives.

- It's easy to find gratitude for the things that provide comfort, ease or beauty. A host of other situations are more challenging. Yet, clarity may arise from pain, learning may come from mistakes, and growth may come from difficulty. Consider problems as opportunities to stretch and be creative. Giving thanks for all kinds of life events reminds you of the potential good in just about everything—*if* you can cultivate an "attitude of gratitude" and allow yourself to see more fully.

- Write about what you have learned from a difficult situation. Is there a lesson or wisdom here that you would want to impart to loved ones? Consider writing a letter to someone with whom you might want to share your insights.

"In ordinary life we hardly realize that we receive a great deal more than we give, and that it is only with gratitude that life becomes rich."
—DIETRICH BONHOEFFER

Waking up this morning,
I see the blue sky.
I join my hands in thanks
For the many wonders of life
For having twenty-four brand new hours
before me.
—THICH NHAT HANH

Yes

It could happen any time, tornado,
earthquake, Armageddon. It could happen.
Or sunshine, love, salvation.

It could, you know. That's why we wake
and look out—no guarantees
in this life.

But some bonuses, like morning,
like right now, like noon,
like evening.

—WILLIAM STAFFORD

Thanks

Listen
with the night falling we are saying thank you
we are stopping on the bridges to bow from the railings
we are running out of the glass rooms
with our mouths full of food to look at the sky
and say thank you
we are standing by the water thanking it
smiling by the windows looking out
in our directions

back from a series of hospitals back from a mugging
after funerals we are saying thank you
after the news of the dead
whether or not we knew them we are saying thank you

over telephones we are saying thank you
in doorways and in the backs of cars and in elevators
remembering wars and the police at the door
and the beatings on stairs we are saying thank you
in the banks we are saying thank you
in the faces of the officials and the rich
and of all who will never change
we go on saying thank you thank you

with the animals dying around us
taking our feelings we are saying thank you
with the forests falling faster than the minutes
of our lives we are saying thank you
with the words going out like cells of a brain
with the cities growing over us
we are saying thank you faster and faster
with nobody listening we are saying thank you
thank you we are saying and waving
dark though it is

—W.S. MERWIN

"There are only two ways to live your life. One is as though nothing is a miracle. The other is as though everything is a miracle."

—ALBERT EINSTEIN

CLOSING MEDITATION

May I be open to the good

May I accept what is

May I remember to give thanks

May I find inner peace

CHAPTER SIX

ON HOPE

"THE FIRST thing I hoped for when I became sick was that I would recover. When, several years into my illness, I realized that wouldn't happen, I hoped that I would live to see my children grow up. When I realized that wasn't going to happen either, I couldn't hold onto a hope that had meaning to me," James, a father of two who was diagnosed with lung cancer in his 30s, told our writing group. "But, much to my surprise, I discovered that being hopeless didn't suit me. With so many things so bleak, I found that I needed to hope about something. Some days it's hoping I can eat breakfast with my wife and kids. Other times I hope that I will be able to read to my children before they go to sleep. At times it's just hoping that I won't give up hope. It's a day-by-day experience and, to be honest, I never thought about hope in these terms—but doing so helps."

"There is a saying in Tibetan, 'Tragedy should be utilized as a source of strength.'

No matter what sort of difficulties, how painful experience is, if we lose our hope, that's our real disaster."

—HIS HOLINESS THE DALAI LAMA

REFLECTIONS ABOUT HOPE

"While there's life, there's hope."

—CICERO

We all want to hope. We want to believe that what we hope for can happen and trust that, in some inexplicable way, our hope will come true. Without hope, it's easy to fall into despair, unable to see what is possible in front of us.

But now, you might well ask, "How does hope play a part in my life when I am living with a life-threatening illness?" Maybe you can no longer hope for a full recovery. Perhaps you realize that it is unlikely you will live to see whatever next life passages will occur in your family such as the growth of your children, future graduations, or becoming a grandparent or great grandparent.

The ways that you understood hope earlier in your life don't feel so comforting or relevant now. But hope is adaptable; it is not static.

This may be hard to realize when you are bombarded by sugarcoated images of hope. The song "Over the Rainbow" is an example. Is the singer really speaking to you? What could you possibly hope for at this point in your life? How do you hope?

Kaethe Weingarten, a writer and psychologist who has struggled with life-threatening illnesses herself, uses the phrase "reasonable hope."[4] Instead of "big" hopes, she concerns herself with more modest hopes about what is possible right now—even in the face of severe illness. She says that reasonable hope, with its acceptance of contradictions and conflicting feelings, offers a platform on which to stand, even when you cannot bear what you must carry.

Perhaps the doctor told you that she does not feel that there is much more she can do to cure you or extend your life. In the face of such devastating news, you might, understandably, rail because it is not what you wanted to hear.

Still, in the worst times, there is always something for which we can hope. You can hope to do a couple of important things before you can no longer do them. A first step might be a family conversation about where you want to spend your last days, how to meet family members' needs and how to deal with financial concerns. There are gentler hopes as well. You can hope to watch a favorite movie. You can hope to listen to music. You can hope to make someone laugh.

Maintaining reasonable hope calls you back to the present moment and your situation, just as it is. Accepting disability or death does not banish reasonable hope. You can set aside what you wish for (those "Over the Rainbow" desires) and hope with humility for what is possible. Reasonable hope invites you to make intentions about how you wish to live and be, no matter how life is unfolding. It invites you to return, again and again, to these intentions, even when things are hard.

Reasonable hope will help you thrive in the face of uncertainty. It accepts that the way ahead is open and uncertain. No one knows the future but you can make choices now that influence how the future may unfold. You can take steps toward whatever outcome you wish for to allow the possibility, and not the probability, that this outcome will occur.

Reasonable hope has "soft" boundaries. It accommodates doubt, contradiction and despair. It will allow you to hold misery and optimism simultaneously without having to choose one over the other or think in black-and-white terms. Shutting down any feelings or suppressing any part of yourself isn't necessary.

Ask other people to join you in holding onto reasonable hope; you don't have to shoulder everything you feel by yourself. You can join with family members, caregivers and friends in a hope that is communal. Reasonable hope is a way of saying, "Yes!" to whatever the roll of life's dice gives you, no matter how great the odds.

"We must accept finite disappointment, but never lose infinite hope."

—REVEREND DR. MARTIN
LUTHER KING, JR.

AN INVITATION TO REFLECT AND WRITE

"Hope is necessary in every condition."
—SAMUEL JOHNSON

A gentle reminder: You don't have to answer all the questions or do all the exercises. Simply choose one or two that resonates with you, work with it for a while, and then rest.

We have all have had different attitudes, experiences and relationship to the concept of hope.

- Are you a hopeful person? Does hope come easily to you? What beliefs do you hold about it? How do you respond to the idea of "reasonable hope"?
- What memories help you sustain a hopeful mindset? Did your children do something that showed you how strong they were? Did your partner complete a task you never imagined possible? Did a friend achieve something, defying great odds? Did your own behavior ever pleasantly surprise you?
- One way to cultivate reasonable hope is by creating a daily practice.
- Imagine starting your day with a hopeful heart.
- What are some reasonable hopes you might harbor right now?
- What might you hope for today?
- Looking beyond this day, what might you reasonably hope for while you are alive and after you have passed?

In writing about reasonable hopes, it is helpful to use short, positive phrases. Here are a few examples of hopes that members of a writing group I worked with shared:

- I hope my nurse knows how much I appreciate what she does for me.
- I hope my sister likes the scrapbook I made for her.
- I hope to die comfortably at home.
- I hope I will not die alone.
- I hope my letters to my children will help them remember me.

We are less lonely if we feel that other people are helping us hold onto our hopes.

- Are there people who are already playing this important role?
- Are there others you would like to ask?
- Would you be willing to consider writing them a letter?

Some common feelings that may accompany reasonable hope include skepticism, despair, doubt, lack of faith and fear. Unlike hope, which tends to be more black-and-white (i.e. you either have it or you don't), reasonable hope is more gray and diffuse.

- Are there other feelings that arise for you around the idea of reasonable hope?
- What might they be?
- Are you still able to hold onto reasonable hope?

"Hope is definitely not the same thing as optimism. It is not the conviction that something will turn out well, but the certainty that something makes sense, regardless of how it turns out."

—VACLAV HAVEL

For the New Year, 1981

I have a small grain of hope—
one small crystal that gleams
clear colors out of transparency.

I need more.
I break off a fragment
to send you.

Please take
this grain of a grain of hope
so that mine won't shrink.

Please share your fragment
so that yours will grow.

Only so, by division,
will hope increase,

like a clump of irises, which will cease to flower
unless you distribute
the clustered roots, unlikely source—
clumsy and earth-covered—
of grace.

—DENISE LEVERTOV

Hope and Love

All winter
the blue heron
slept among the horses.
I do not know
the custom of herons,
do not know
if the solitary habit
is their way,
or if he listened for
some missing one—
not knowing even
that was what he did—
in the blowing
sounds in the dark.
I know that
hope is the hardest
love we carry.
He slept
with his long neck
folded, like a letter
put away.

—JANE HIRSCHFIELD

"The very least you can do in your life is to figure out what to hope for. And the most you can do is live inside that hope."

—BARBARA KINGSOLVER

CLOSING MEDITATION

May I be free of fear

May I find strength for my journey

May I be guided by reasonable hope

May I find inner peace

CHAPTER SEVEN

ON FORGIVENESS

"I AM ONE of those people who holds a grudge. I remember every slight, every time I felt used or disrespected. It's not a happy way to live, but I couldn't help it," Joan, an 83-year-old woman with end-stage cancer, shared with our writing group. "I felt angry with others and even more angry with myself for letting those situations affect me so deeply. And yet I couldn't let them go. Finally, with so little time left, I realized that holding those grudges took too much energy. And, if I was to be honest with myself, I knew that I did things to people that they, in turn, probably held against me. Forgiveness is not, for me, an easy thing. Forgiving myself is hardest of all. But I do want to put these bad feelings to rest and writing about them helped me. Remember that old saying, 'You can't take it with you?' Maybe, in addition to material things, it also refers to anger and grudges and resentments."

REFLECTIONS ABOUT FORGIVENESS

"To forgive is to set a prisoner free and discover the prisoner was you."

—UNKNOWN

Learning to forgive and practicing forgiveness plays a central role in all the major religious and spiritual traditions. In the secular realm, too, researchers have studied the positive benefits of forgiveness. The experience of forgiving, it turns out, decreases anger and lessens depression, anxiety and stress. It also increases our overall sense of well-being.

So what do we mean when we talk about forgiveness? Forgiving means letting go of anger and blame. It is a commitment to understanding, more deeply and with greater empathy, the complex situations that develop between people. At the same time, we recognize that forgiving is not forgetting, condoning, excusing, trusting without reason, or reconciling in the face of potential danger.

With forgiveness, we give up hope of changing the past. We abandon our right to resentment and judgment, and try to find some of the not-so-positive qualities in our self that we ascribe to the "other" person. Most importantly, forgiving means that we acknowledge our common imperfect humanity as we look more closely at ourselves and see that we are not so different from other people. Forgiveness begins with ourselves.

Reflecting on relationships over the course of our life prompts us to remember all the things we said and did, things that we now regret. We hurt others through our speech and actions, carelessness and neglect, anger or gossip. Sometimes when we were really angry, we probably even intended to harm. We have also injured ourselves through harsh self-criticism, by not taking care of our bodies, or by allowing others to act in hurtful ways toward us.

How do we begin to forgive ourselves? How do we admit to ourselves that we did something wrong? How do we tolerate cracks in our self-image? How do we see ourselves in a new light? Saying "I am sorry" can leave us feeling tender, open and vulnerable. Sometimes we may find ourselves in unfamiliar territory and outside our comfort zone.

This is a time to be kind to yourself—to gather your courage and energy and begin anew. When you look back at difficult moments from your life, you can see how you were always acting from, and within, a particular set of circumstances. At any moment, you only knew so much. You were limited in different ways. Looking back, you might feel that you could or should have done better or differently, but you didn't. Consider that you did the very best you could at that particular time.

How do you work with mistakes and hurtful words or actions? How do you use them to both humble yourself and open your heart a little bit wider? Are you able to see how much like everyone else you are, that every person suffers in similar ways? Are you willing to look closely at yourself with kindness so you can grow wiser?

How do you begin to make amends when you have hurt someone else? Consider writing a letter, taking responsibility for what you have said or done. Just writing to someone will lighten your load. By writing, you will free yourself by letting go of carrying the heavy baggage of regret and shame. Writing can close unfinished business. Writing can also help you to remember that you are not perfect and help you find inner peace.

In writing—or even thinking about writing to another person— you let go of the desire that you can influence or change his or her feelings or responses. You may even decide not to mail the letter. That is not what is most important. What matters is that you write with words that will do no harm. You write so that your remaining days are less encumbered by regrets and unspoken words. By writing you take full responsibility for your actions. You leave a legacy that opens a path toward healing for all of you.

"Forgiving is not forgetting; it's letting go of the hurt."
—MARY MCLEOD BETHUNE

AN INVITATION TO REFLECT AND WRITE

"You will know that forgiveness has begun when you recall those who hurt you and feel the power to wish them well."

—C.S. LEWIS

A gentle resminder: You don't have to answer all the questions or do all the exercises. Simply choose one or two that resonates with you, work with it for a while, and then rest.

Think about apologizing

- Who are some of the people in your life to whom you might want to offer an apology? People you choose do not have to be living.
- Is there one person in particular with whom you could start?

Consider what harms you perceive occurred between you

- Is there a letter you could write to that person in which you take responsibility for your actions, being truthful and offering an apology? Remember, you are not asking for the other's forgiveness but simply taking responsibility for your own actions.

As you think about writing something, you might want to consider some of the following questions to remind you to be compassionate with yourself

- What was the context of your life when this conflict occurred?
- How might your childhood experiences have contributed to this situation?
- Where were you living? What were your relationships like at that time? Where were you working?
- What was your emotional state?
- As you remember these events, can you remember ways in which you were suffering and in need of healing?
- Could you extend some empathy for yourself as you reflect?
- What are your recollections of the event in which you feel that you acted in ways that caused suffering to another?
- For what exactly do you want to apologize?

After you have written one letter, consider whether there is another one that you might write.

> *"We are all full of weakness and errors; let us mutually pardon each other our follies."*
>
> —VOLTAIRE

Late August

It's as if we're always preparing
for something, the endless roll of the earth
ripening us.
Even on the most tranquil
late August afternoon when heavy heads
of phlox bow in the garden
and the hummingbird sits still for a moment
on a branch of an apple tree—
even on such a day,
evening approaches sooner
than yesterday, and we cannot help
noticing whole families of birds
arrive together in the enclosure,
young blue birds molted a misty grey,
colored through no will of their own
for a journey.
On such an evening
I ache for what I cannot keep—the birds,
the phlox, the late-flying bees—
though I would not forbid the frost,
even if I could. There will be more to love
and lose in what's to come and this too: desire
to see it clear before it's gone.

—MARY CHIVERS

The Bodies of Grownups

The bodies of grownups
come with stretch marks and scars,
faces that have been lived in,
relaxed breasts and bellies
backs that give trouble,
and well-worn feet:
flesh that is particular,
and obviously mortal.
They also come
with bruises on their hearts,
wounds they can't forget,
and each of them
a company of lovers in their soul
who will not return
and cannot be erased.
And yet I think there is a flood of beauty
beyond the smoothness of youth;
and my heart aches for that grace of longing
that flows through bodies
no longer straining to be innocent,
but yearning for redemption.

—JANET MORLEY

Acceptance

When your past
comes to live
in the woods
behind your house,
you must go
to the window,
forgive yourself
once again,
and welcome
the creature
that suns himself
on the sill.

—NANCY COMPTON WILLIAMS

"The weak can never forgive. Forgiveness is the attribute of the strong."

—MAHATMA GANDHI

CLOSING MEDITATION

May I forgive myself for the harm I have done to others,
knowingly and unknowingly
May I forgive others the harm done to me,
knowingly or unknowingly
May I forgive myself for the harm I have done to myself,
knowingly and unknowingly
May I forgive myself for what I am yet unable to forgive.

CHAPTER EIGHT

ON WISDOM

Nancy was a 75-year-old woman who lived in a residential hospice. During my visits, she repeatedly recounted a conversation with her psychiatrist after she was diagnosed with cancer. She asked him how she would know when to stop fighting for her life. Dr. Z's response was, "Of all my patients, you, above all, will know." Nancy was perplexed by his answer and did not know what he had seen in her that would lead him to make such a comment. One day I suggested that she write him a letter. That's what she did, and Dr. Z responded within 24 hours. This is what he wrote:

Dear Nancy:

Thank you for asking. I have been deeply moved by the grace and wisdom with which you have brought together faith, hope, clinical data, humor, music and resolve each step of the way from the time you first received the diagnosis of a life-threatening illness to the present. You have managed to find within you the right response at the right time throughout each chapter and even the perfect pictures to put up on your walls when you moved back to Massachusetts. You are not only my patient, but a special person and a unique role model I will continue to learn from.

I always look forward to our next conversation.

JZ

REFLECTIONS ABOUT WISDOM

"True wealth is not measured in money or status or power. It is measured in the legacy we leave behind for those we love and those we inspire."

—CESAR CHAVEZ

As we begin to close our lives, most of us want to find ways of sharing what we learned with other people. What are the essential lessons of your life? How did you learn them? How will you pass them on?

One way is by writing an ethical will. Historically, ethical wills were ancient documents that were common in both the Jewish and Christian traditions. These documents, referred to in the Old Testament and often written from fathers to sons, were intended for private use. They were designed to help transmit values from one generation to another. In more recent times, they have become documents used by everyone, and while they are not "official or binding" in the way that legal wills are, they are important in different ways.

Ethical wills typically describe your values. For example, they can include blessings that you would like to confer on others, lessons you have learned through your life and whatever dreams you may have for your loved ones in the future. Some of the commonly expressed values include the importance of family and friends, generosity, education, hard work and kindness. By becoming clear about your values, it's possible to realize their importance in shaping your life. It's not surprising, therefore, to want others to know that about yourself and desire that those values be passed on. They are intangible heirlooms to be cherished.

Here is an excerpt of an ethical will from a young mother to her children:

Dear D and T:

As I have thought about my dying and leaving the two of you, it has been very difficult to imagine your lives without me. I want to thank you both for the joy you have brought into my life as a mother and share with you a few lessons I have learned in my dying. While you are too young right now to understand them, I have asked Dad to put this ethical will away until you are a little more grown up.

I have learned in my dying that nothing is more important than love. During much of my short life, I tended to be harsh with myself, to be judgmental. Remember to be patient with the parts of your selves that you don't like. Be kind to yourselves, to one another and other people. Everyone is doing the best that they know how. Patience has become very important to me. It's not at all easy to be patient but it is something that I have learned through my cancer. Nothing is more important than loving one another and helping each other.

When you think of me, try to remember to love.

I love you so,
Mom

As you compose the will, you may discover that your core values and life lessons came out of a difficult experience. When you reflect on your life lessons, you might see that your greatest teacher was your own pain and suffering. With an open mind and an undefended heart, you come to understand that all experiences are opportunities for learning.

Being able to face the times when you suffered is enormously challenging. You may again feel vulnerable, feel the sting of regret or shame. You likely want to flee from these memories. But if you are able to linger with them, you will see how you survived. You will come to know your strengths.

In the crucible of reflection, suffering transforms into compassion and wisdom. You learn that—even at this late hour—you acquired hard-won experience and wisdom to pass on. Sharing this wisdom is a way to offer comfort, help and guidance to those left behind. When you write from your heart, wisdom naturally arises.

Do you remember instructions or guidance you received from your family, community or religious affiliation when you were young? Perhaps these values were imparted very directly while at other times you might have learned them by reading between the lines of what your parents said or what your religion taught. Some examples of guidance are:

- Keep a stiff upper lip
- Maintain peace at any price
- Do unto others as you would have them do unto you
- Nothing is more important than education

You probably now have your own ethical beliefs or guidance that you would like to pass on, lessons from your own life that you would like others to know. These teachings may be similar to, or different from, the ones you were given. Consider for a moment what some of those might be. As you think about them and begin to write them down, consider phrases that are short, simple and positive. That way, your loved ones may be more able to receive them. Here are some examples:

- "Be generous with others" instead of "Don't hoard your money"
- "Take into consideration the needs of others" rather than "Don't be selfish all the time"
- "What is most essential in life is how you live, not what you acquire" versus "Material things won't bring happiness"

Another approach (since none of us likes to be told what to do) is to offer blessings. By simply changing the wording on an instruction, the tone changes and an instruction becomes a blessing. Remember, as author Rachel Remen says, offering a blessing is touching the "unborn goodness" in the other.[5] Here are some examples:

- "May you find joy in giving" versus "Be generous with another"
- "May you come to know the satisfaction in non-material things" versus "Buying things won't bring you ultimate happiness"
- "May you be blessed, as I have been, with a strong active body" versus "Work to stay in shape, so that you are healthy"

By using blessing types of words such as, "May you find . . ." or "My deepest wish for you is that . . . " or "In my love for you, may you find . . ." the messages are more apt to be received.

These wishes for goodness are from your heart to the hearts of those you love. As you come to the end of your life, you may find you want to reach into that goodness and share it with others.

"With each blessing uttered we extend the boundaries of the sacred and ritualize our love of life."

—Lawrence Kushner

AN INVITATION TO REFLECT AND WRITE

"Wisdom is a living stream, not an icon preserved in a museum. Only when we find the spring of wisdom in our own life can it flow to future generations."

—THICH NHAT HANH

A gentle reminder: You don't have to answer all the questions or do all exercises. Simply choose one or two that resonates with you, work with it for a while, and then rest.

Choose an instruction/blessing that was a lesson learned through pain and suffering

- Do you remember how you learned this lesson?
- Do you know why it is so important to you to want to pass it on?
- Is there a story behind your learning it that you might share?

Is there one lesson or piece of guidance that feels especially important to you to pass onto loved ones or future generations?

- Write it out as an instruction. Re-write it as a blessing, using the tips on the previous pages to change the tone.
- Have you actually written a blessing well or have you re-written an instruction or lesson? (This is surprisingly easy to do.) You may choose to ask others to describe to you what tone they hear in what you have written so that you can judge whether your words adequately convey your meaning.

- Imagine if you were the recipient of this lesson. How do you think you might respond?

The following is an example from one of my workshops

- The writer began with an instruction:

  "Be generous."

- She then rewrote it in the form of a blessing:

  "May you always be guided through life by generosity and the capacity to give without having to be known for your gifts."

- The writer amplified her blessing with this story, writing from the strength of her vulnerability:

  "One of the things your grandfather used to do was to donate to charities anonymously. I always thought he was quite special for doing that, but I had not yet learned the wisdom of that gesture. As I grew older, I did some very part time work for a non-profit caring for people with cancer. At the end of the week, I would give them back my compensation as a donation toward the work they were doing. I enjoyed the gratitude that came my way. When I left that group to work more locally, I stopped donating to them.

  A couple of years later, I received a phone call from the Executive Director, asking me to return to do some more work for them. I wondered to myself whether they were asking me back because of my skill set or because they wanted me to resume my donations to them. That persistent question led me, as your grandfather did, to give anonymously when I made donations. Now I feel that there is more separation and clarity between my work life and my philanthropy."

• Do you want to share other life lessons or offer another blessing?

"Give sorrow words. The grief that does not speak whispers the o'er-fraught heart, and bids it break."

—SHAKESPEARE

The Guest House

This being human is a guest house.
Every morning a new arrival.

A joy, a depression, a meanness,
some momentary awareness comes
as an unexpected visitor.

Welcome and entertain them all!
Even if they are a crowd of sorrows,
who violently sweep your house
empty of its furniture,
still, treat each guest honorably.
He may be clearing you out
for some new delight.

The dark thought, the shame, the malice,
meet them at the door laughing,
and invite them in.

Be grateful for whoever comes,
because each has been sent
as a guide from beyond.

—JELALUDDIN RUMI

The Unbroken

There is a brokenness
out of which comes the unbroken,
a shatteredness
out of which blooms the unshatterable.

There is a sorrow
beyond all grief which leads to joy
and a fragility
out of whose depths emerges strength.

There is a hollow space
too vast for words
through which we pass with each loss,
out of whose darkness
we are sanctioned into being.

There is a cry deeper than all sound
whose serrated edges cut the heart
as we break open to the place inside
which is unbreakable and whole,
while learning to sing.

—RASHANI RÉA

"The world is waiting for us to bless it."
—NAOMI LEVY

CLOSING MEDITATION

May I be free of suffering

May I be compassionate with myself

May my life help others

May I find inner peace

CHAPTER NINE

ON PRAYER

JOHN, A member of my writing group, wrote the following: "I was raised a Catholic, and was always an active member of the church when I was a little kid. I was even an altar boy as a teenager. But when I went to college, something happened and I began to doubt everything I had been taught. I stopped going to church and really had questions about God and prayer. At 24, I got leukemia and was in the hospital for many weeks. I had to have a stem cell transplant and was isolated for a long time. There was plenty of time to look out the window at a tree. Over several weeks I watched the tree grow more and more beautiful. The leaves changed colors from green to yellow to red and then gradually fell to the ground. There was something about watching all this that, even though I had lost my faith in prayer, seemed to open up my heart and mind to the possibility of a connection to something larger than myself. I remember thinking to myself, 'I hope to be so beautiful as I fall.' It all seemed like a prayer to me."

REFLECTIONS ABOUT PRAYER

"The urge to pray is universal."

—THICH NHAT HANH

In the face of life-threatening illness, many people turn to prayer. Up against sickness and the fear of dying, the need to search for something that might help you walk toward the unknown, to connect with something larger than yourself, is understandable. How you pray is unique to you. Maybe you have been praying since you were a child. Perhaps you were never taught to pray. Possibly you tried prayer, and it didn't seem helpful. Maybe you even felt betrayed because your prayers did not seem to be answered. And now you need help.

How do you feel about prayer?

Anne Lamott, in her book *Help, Thanks, Wow*, writes that prayer, regardless of its form, may be as simple and as profound as a cry for help. She describes prayer as a "communication from the heart to that which surpasses understanding."[6] It expresses our yearning to be heard; it is a call out into silence, a cry to be united with some larger force than ourselves, a cry from deep within to life or love. Prayer is a wish to believe that we are loved despite whatever we have done, and to hope for something larger than our self to intervene and journey with us in the face of the myriad losses we experience as we approach the end of our life.

Saying yes to your need for help becomes the start of a prayer. Once you are oriented toward prayer, you may find it in writing, singing, dancing, looking at the sun or watching the movement of branches in a tree. It may be a moment of listening to music, or watching a sunset from your bedroom window that moves you. Or it might be a quiet moment with a loved one, the nurse who is caring for you or a pet. Prayer is a quality of openness to the moment, to what is within, to your deepest yearnings, to your need to be heard, to be loved and to be helped.

> *"Prayer is an act of love, words are not needed. Even if sickness distracts thoughts, all that is needed is the will to love."*
>
> —St. Teresa of Avila

AN INVITATION TO REFLECT AND WRITE

*"Each time we acknowledge that we aren't doing any of
this alone and then write or talk to someone else about
what is going on inside us, we are offering up a prayer."*
—NANCY O'HARA

A gentle reminder: You don't have to answer all the questions or do all
the exercises. Simply choose one or two that resonate with you, work
with it for a while, and then rest.

Gathering prayers

- What messages were you given in your childhood about prayer?
  What prayers were you taught and which of those have you
  continued to say?
- What writings have been sacred scriptures or writings for you?
  They might include formal prayers, meditations, poetry or even
  literature.
- If you were writing a prayer that you felt would be received
  by someone who loved you unconditionally and could really
  hear the deepest yearnings of your heart, what might you say to
  that person? Can you write a prayer, without holding back any
  reservation, asking for the specific help that you feel you need?
  If you are able to write it out, read it over to see whether the
  prayer offers you the comfort you are seeking.

• Each of us has a unique expression of prayer. It might be through poetry, movement or stillness or through images of art or music. It might occur when visitors are with you or when you are alone. What are some of the ways that you have felt open to something larger than yourself? Let those forms of prayer move through you.

"When you cannot pray as you would, pray as you can."

—DEAN M. GOULBURN

I Was Never Able To Pray

Wheel me down to the shore
where the lighthouse was abandoned
and the moon tolls in the rafters.

Let me hear the wind paging through the trees
and see the stars flaring out, one by one,
like the forgotten faces of the dead.

I was never able to pray,
but let me inscribe my name
in the book of waves

and then stare into the dome
of a sky that never ends
and see my voice sail into the night.

—EDWARD HIRSCH

If Prayer Would Do It

If prayer would do it
I'd pray.

If reading esteemed thinkers would do it
I'd be halfway through the Patriarchs.

If discourse would do it
I'd be sitting with His Holiness
every moment he was free.

If contemplation would do it
I'd have translated the Periodic Table
to hermit poems, converting
matter to spirit.

If even fighting would do it
I'd already be a black belt.

If anything other than love could do it
I've done it already
and left the hardest for last.

—STEPHEN LEVINE

"Each one prays to God according to his own light."
—MAHATMA GANDHI

CLOSING MEDITATION

May I be open to praying

May I find comfort in my prayer(s)

May I feel heard

May I feel loved

CHAPTER TEN

ON ENDINGS

After participating in our writing group, George, a man in his fifties, decided the time had come to talk to his wife, Nina, about his death. He called her to his bedside and opened up the conversation by saying, "This is not easy to say, but I have wanted to talk with you for so long about the fact that I know I am going to die soon. I want for us to start to make some plans for this together. I need to know that you and the children will be cared for. I want to write down what needs to be done. I want to leave words that will live on after I'm gone."

REFLECTIONS ABOUT ENDINGS

"Death ends a life, not a relationship."
—ROBERT BENCHLEY

It is not easy to initiate a conversation about hopes and wishes at the end of life. We fear pain and suffering and loss. We face an uncertain journey. Many of our ideas and images about death and dying are unexamined, negative, and sometimes even terrifying.

It is difficult to acknowledge, even to ourselves, that we are reaching the end of our lives. How do we find the words to tell our loved ones what is on our minds? How do the people around us hear us speaking frankly about how we want to conclude our lives?

Before you became sick maybe you had trouble expressing your feelings and wishes. Now that you are ill and more is at stake, speaking up may be harder still. It is common to feel that serious discussions will upset family members. Loved ones may be reluctant to engage in these discussions for fear of upsetting you. Perhaps you fear that by entering into these end-of-life conversations, you are somehow giving up or hastening death. Some part of you knows that this is not true, but this worry still holds you back. It might be comforting to know that there is research that suggests that starting palliative care, such as hospice, and having these kinds of conversations, has been shown to result in longer life, less depression and a higher quality of life for those with advanced disease.[7]

As challenging as this time might be, it offers a precious opportunity to reflect on your ideas about death and dying. Doing so offers the opportunity to (metaphorically speaking) plant new seeds and to re-image or re-imagine old ideas you picked up from the culture. This is your chance—in these fleeting days and moments—to summon your courage and acknowledge what you believe and want and then share those thoughts about death and dying with family and loved ones. When you find ways to share what is on your mind, you are often giving a gift both to yourself and to the people around you.

Some of the questions you may want to reflect upon as you move toward the end of your life might include

- What beliefs you have
- What kinds of care you want
- How you wish to spend the last few days
- What you would like done with your body after you have died
- How you imagine your funeral or memorial service will be or if you prefer neither one

There is a booklet available on the Internet called *Five Wishes*, which may be very helpful in thinking through many of these end-of-life issues. The booklet includes places in which you can write out all your preferences and share them with your loved ones.[8]

But how do you initiate these intimate exchanges about end-of-life desires? One way, especially if you are worried about how others will respond to a conversation, is to write a letter that offers a little space and time between you and loved ones. That way, they may consider your words and think them over before reacting or responding. You might want to write a letter to your children that shares your dreams for them and their future lives. Or perhaps there is some guidance or wisdom that you wish to share that came out of a painful or personal experience you lived through. Perhaps you want to let your partner know that you hope he or she finds companionship after you are gone.

What about opening a conversation? One way to begin is by saying, "I've been thinking about what I would want when I become gravely ill or if I were to die suddenly. I want to share my thinking with you." Samuel Bojar wrote his ideal end-of-life plan in a booklet called "Just in Case" and updates it for his family.[9] Or you may choose a more direct approach.

An invaluable resource for helping you find more ways to initiate these conversations is available through The Conversation Project, which was founded by Ellen Goodman, a Pulitzer Prize winning columnist. The web site offers a Starter Kit which you can download for free, and offers a variety of additional ideas and support for beginning a conversation about your wishes at the end of life with loved ones. [10]

As you come to the end of your life, you are preparing for the final good-bye. You can no longer realistically say, "See you later" or "I am sure we will meet up again" or any one of the other phrases used in our culture that keep us from really saying "good-bye."

Yet grasping the reality of the end offers a beautiful opening within yourself, as well as with others. Maybe you have already observed that among those for whom death is in close sight, there is often an intense vitality, aliveness and awareness of the preciousness of this fleeting moment. It is bittersweet that in close proximity to death, it is possible to feel most alive. In the remarkable documentary "Griefwalker" there is a line that explains the thought so well: "The crucible of making human beings is death, not happiness. That is the cradle of your love of life."[11]

May you find and be upheld in that love. May your lasting words serve to help you feel that you belong, that you are known and remembered, that your life made a difference. May they bless you and allow you to be blessed. May they celebrate your life.

> *"I've learned that people will forget what you said, people will forget what you did, but people will never forget how you made them feel."*
>
> —MAYA ANGELOU

AN INVITATION TO REFLECT AND WRITE

> *"Love is stronger than death even though it can't stop death from happening, but no matter how hard death tries it can't separate people from love. It can't take away our memories either. In the end, life is stronger than death."*
>
> —UNKNOWN

A gentle reminder: You don't have to answer all the questions or do all the exercises. Simply choose one or two that resonates with you, work with it for a while, and then rest.

Some of the writing exercises that follow are designed to help you closely consider how to spend your last days. They can help you to explore your ideas about death with an eye to helping you articulate your preferences as you grow sicker. The last set of questions is aimed at helping you contribute to your funeral or memorial service.

Considering your last days

- What concerns do you have about your health or future health care needs?
- What in your life is most important and meaningful right now?
- Is there anything that you have yet to say or do that would bring about completion with a loved one or friend?
- Is there anything you still want to accomplish?
- If you could plan it today, what would the last day of your life be like?
- Where would you go?
- What would you do?
- With whom would you share this time?
- Would you want to make a final visit to a special place, family or friends?

Looking at death

- When you think about death, what kinds of images, thoughts and feelings come up for you? What do you think influenced these ideas? Did they come from literature, films, television, religion, family or friends?
- What parts of dying feel frightening to you? Do you know the source of these fearful thoughts?
- What positive images, impressions, or ideas do you carry that will help you deal with dying in an open and receptive way?
- What reasonable hopes are you carrying?

Imagining your death

- What music do you imagine you would most like to hear?
- What words would provide a source of comfort (prayers, passages, psalms, poetry, etc.)?
- What belongings do you want nearby, either to see, or touch or smell?
- What would be the ideal physical surrounding for you in the end?
- Whom do you imagine you would most want to be near you?
- Are there words you would want to say to those at your bedside, or words you would like to hear from them?
- Are there circumstances under which you would refuse or discontinue treatment that might prolong your life? If so, what are they?
- Would you want to have a hospice team or other palliative (comfort) care available to you? Would you prefer a residential hospice (if available)? What would your preferences be if you were incapable of making a decision for yourself about end-of-life treatments?
- What do you think you will need for comfort and support as you live out your last days?
- What do you want to have happen when you die? Are there beliefs about your body, or from your religion/spirituality, that you would like to honor and respect?
- What would you like to have done with your body (charity, cremation, green burial, traditional burial, medical research)?

Imagining your funeral or remembrance

- What kind of funeral service would you like held for you?
- How do you want to be remembered at your service?
- Who would you like to speak on your behalf or offer a eulogy?
- Is there anything in particular you would like for them to say about you?
- If you wrote your own eulogy or obituary, what would it say? Are there parts of it you might want read by someone in particular at your service?
- Are there sections of the service that you would like to plan, such as choosing a poem, or a passage that has been especially important to you?
- Are there favorites hymns or songs you would like played or sung?
- At a gathering, is there special food that you would want to be served, or photographs you would want displayed, that represent important milestones in your life's journey?[12]

"May the long time sun shine upon you, all love surround you, and the pure light within you guide your way on."

—TRADITIONAL BLESSING

Let Evening Come

Let the light of late afternoon
shine through chinks in the barn, moving
up the bales as the sun moves down.

Let the cricket take up chafing
as a woman takes up her needles
and her yarn. Let evening come.

Let dew collect on the hoe abandoned
in long grass. Let the stars appear
and the moon disclose her silver horn.

Let the fox go back to its sandy den.
Let the wind die down. Let the shed
go black inside. Let evening come.

To the bottle in the ditch, to the scoop
in the oats, to air in the lung
let evening come.

Let it come, as it will, and don't
be afraid. God does not leave us
comfortless, so let evening come.

—JANE KENYON

I Am Not I

I am not I.

   I am this one
Walking beside me whom I do not see,
Whom at times I manage to visit,
And whom at other times I forget;
The one who remains silent when I talk,
The one who forgives, sweet, when I hate,
The one who takes a walk where I am not,
The one who will remain standing when I die.

  —Juan Ramón Jiménez

Parable of Immortality

I am standing upon the sea shore.
A ship at my side spreads her white sails to the
morning breeze and starts for the blue ocean.

She is an object of beauty and strength.
I stand and watch her until at length she hangs
like a speck of white cloud just where the sea and sky come
      to mingle with each other.

Then someone at my side says;
"There, she is gone!"
Gone where?

Gone from my sight . . . That is all.

She is just as large in mast and hull and spar
as she was when she left my side
and she is just as able to bear her load of living freight
to her destined port.

Her diminished size is in me, not in her.

And just at that moment when someone at my side says,
"There, she is gone!"
there are other eyes watching her and
other voices ready to take up the glad shout . . .
"Here she comes!"
And that is dying.

    —HENRY VAN DYKE

"When your time comes, may you have
Every blessing and strength you need.

May there be a beautiful welcome for you
In the home you are going to.

You are not going somewhere strange,
Merely back to the home you have never left."
—JOHN O'DONOHUE

CLOSING MEDITATION

May I be free of fear
May I be free of suffering
May I have strength for my journey
May I find inner peace

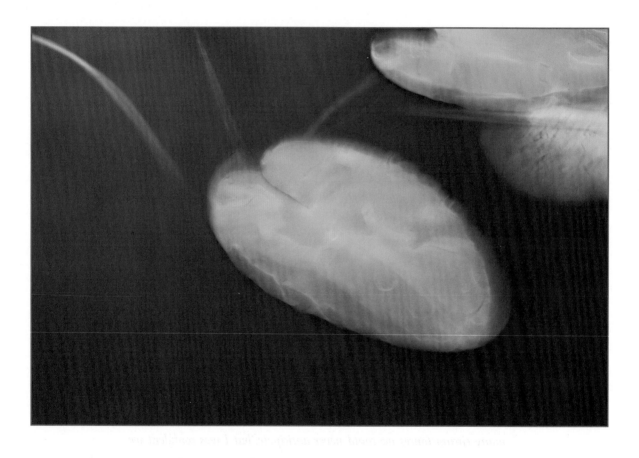

Epilogue

EVERY PERSON'S lasting words are unique. Sam, who joined a bereavement group I was leading shortly after his wife, Sue, died, reinforced this truth. Sue had told Sam that she had written a long letter to Linda, their 10-year-old daughter. When Sam retrieved the letter, he found a second letter written to him. Sam brought it into the bereavement group and shared it with the other members. These are some excerpts from Sue's letter.

January 23, 2011
My dearest Love,

When we dreamed of having a child together, I knew there would be many circumstances we could never anticipate, but I was confident we would figure them out together. Now the unthinkable has happened, leaving you to figure out on your own how to carry on as a single parent. I am so sorry. Even though it's hardly my fault, I feel terrible as I write this, knowing how difficult parenting is, how you struggle with it, and can only imagine the challenges you will face in raising Linda alone.

My intent in writing this is to give you my thoughts on a variety of topics with the hope that I can provide some insight, support, and guidance as you navigate your relationship with our beautiful and amazing daughter. My intent is not to tell you what to do or to hover (metaphorically) over your shoulder, but simply to give you my collected thoughts in the hope that you might find something useful among them. If you find yourself getting agitated while reading this, muttering under your breath at me for telling you things you already know, first forgive me for trying and then read it again and ask yourself if there isn't something worth taking in.

Parent from your heart, as much as from your head, if not more so. One of the many gifts you have brought to our parenting partnership (and our marriage) is your ability to continue thinking rationally in the midst of emotionally laden situations. My fear is that you are so comfortable in rational mode—and so good at it—that at times you put your feelings on the back burner. I often did the opposite, and as long as we were both in the picture we tended to balance each other out. Now Linda needs to get both perspectives from you.

Never forget that you are the adult. Whether that means losing a game graciously, or overlooking hurtful words she may throw at you in anger, rise above it. You have the broader perspective on what's really important. By being the adult in the relationship you allow her to be the child, while also providing her with a model of the kind of behavior that will be expected of her as she matures.

Don't expect perfection from Linda or from yourself. You are notoriously hard on yourself and that tends to seep into your expectations for Linda. Just remember, no matter how smart she is she's still a child (or teen), and while it's appropriate to hold her to high standards because she is so smart and capable, setting those standards unrealistically high will only result in her feeling bad about herself and in unnecessary conflict between the two of you.

Let lots of stuff go. Life is complicated, Linda is complicated, You're both in a tough spot having lost your wife/mother. Before correcting her or nudging her or disciplining her, ask yourself if this one is worth it.

Ask for help when you need it and accept all reasonable offers of help even if you don't absolutely need it at that moment. First of all, you don't get extra brownie points for going it alone. Second, you are doing a mitzvah by letting others do a mitzvah for you. And third, as capable as you are, you can't possibly be all things for Linda all the time.

Let new love into your life. I know this will seem impossible for a long time, but at some point, I want you to open yourself to the possibility of loving someone else. You have so much to give, and I believe that you are at your best when in relationship with someone else. Falling in love again (or forming a partnership based on less intense feelings such as friendship and compatibility) will in no way dishonor my memory or diminish the love we had for each other. In fact, it would honor our partnership and the tremendous growth you made in it, growth which, when you're ready, will give you the strength to reach out again to give and accept love.

SOURCES

1. Rachael Freed. (2012). *Women's lives, Women's Legacies: Passing Your Beliefs and Blessings to Future Generations* (2nd ed.). Minneapolis, MN: Minerva Press.

2. Pema Chodron. (2001). *The Places That Scare You: A Guide to Fearlessness in Difficult Times.* Boston, MA: Shambhala.

3. Rich Hanson. (2011). *Just One Thing.* Oakland, CA: New Harbinger.

4. Kaethe Weingarten. (2010). Reasonable hope: Construct, clinical applications, and supports. *Family Process* 49:5–25.

5. Rachel Naomi Remen. (2001). *My Grandfather's Blessings: Stories of Strength, Refuge, and Belonging.* New York, NY. Riverhead Books. Page 5.

6. Anne Lamott. (2012). *Help, Thanks, Wow: The Three Essential Prayers.* New York: Riverhead Press.

7. Susan Bauer-Wu and Joan Halifax. (2011). *Leaves Falling Gently: Living Fully with Serious and Life-Limiting Illness Through Mindfulness, Compassion, and Connectedness.* Oakland, CA New Harbinger Publications.

8. www.agingwithdignity.org. Phone: 888-594-7437.

9. Barbara Okun and Joseph Nowinski. http://www.health.harvard. edu/blog/end-of-life-planning-makes-it-easier-to-say-goodbye-201101221210

10. www.theconversationproject.org

11. Wilson, T. (2008). *Griefwalker*. USA: Alive Mind.

12. www.ihpco.org/consumer/beginning-conversations-about-end-life-decisions Indiana Hospice and Palliative Care Organization. Many of the questions in this section came from this web site.

ACKNOWLEDGEMENTS

The poems in this book come from copyrighted sources. Permission to use the poems reprinted in this book was granted by the following:

Acceptance
"Acceptance" by Nancy Compton Williams. First appeared in the online journal *Sacred Journey*. Reprinted with permission of the author.

The Bodies of Grownups
"The Bodies of Grownups" from *All Desires Known* by Janet Morley. Copyright © 2006 Published by Morehouse Publishing Inc. Reprinted with permission of Church Publishing, Inc. NY, NY.

For the New Year, 1981
By Denise Levertov, from *Candles in Babylon*. Copyright © 1982 by Denise Levertov. Reprinted by permission of New Directions Publishing Corp.

The Guest House
"The Guest House" from *The Essential Rumi*. Written by Jelaluddin Rumi, translated by Coleman Barks. Reprinted with permission of Coleman Barks.

Hope and Love
"Hope and Love" from *The Lives of the Heart* by Jane Hirshfield. Copyright © 1997 by Jane Hirshfield. Reprinted by permission of HarperCollins Publishers.